PHOTOGRAPHIC MEMORY

Can your brain click pictures?

V. Aishwaryalakshmi

Copyright © 2023 V. Aishwaryalakshmi

All rights reserved

No part of this book may be reproduced, or stored in a retrieval system, or transmitted in any form or by any means, electronic, mechanical, photocopying, recording, or otherwise, without express written permission of the publisher.

CONTENTS

Title Page
Copyright
Preface
CHAPTER 1 — 2
CHAPTER 2 — 4
CHAPTER 3 — 9
CHAPTER 4 — 13
CHAPTER 5 — 17
CHAPTER 6 — 19
CHAPTER 7 — 21
CHAPTER 8 — 23
CHAPTER 9 — 25
CHAPTER 10 — 28
CHAPTER 11 — 32
CHAPTER 12 — 36
CHAPTER 13 — 39
CHAPTER 14 — 41
CHAPTER 15 — 44
About The Author — 46

PREFACE

I have always been fascinated by the power of the human mind to capture and retain images with incredible detail and clarity. Our brains have the amazing ability to store vast amounts of visual information, allowing us to recall even the tiniest details of a scene long after it has disappeared from view. This ability is commonly known as photographic memory, and it is a subject that has captivated scientists, psychologists, and everyday people alike for decades.

In this book, I delve into the fascinating world of photographic memory, exploring what it is, how it works, and how it can be developed. I also provide practical tips and techniques for improving your memory and enhancing your ability to recall images with stunning clarity.

Whether you are a student, a professional, or simply someone who wants to better understand the mysteries of the human mind, this book is for you. So join me on a journey of discovery as we explore the incredible power of photographic memory and unlock the full potential of our minds.

Contents

1. What is Photographic Memory and How Does it Work
2. Types of Photographic Memory
3. How to Develop a Photographic Memory
4. Techniques to Improve Your Photographic Memory
5. Memory Palace: A Technique for Remembering Anything
6. Mnemonic Devices for Memorization
7. How to Remember Names and Faces
8. How to Remember Dates and Numbers
9. How to Remember Text and Information
10. Photographic Memory and Education
11. Photographic Memory and Career Advancement
12. The Science Behind Photographic Memory
13. World Records done using Photographic Memory
14. Myths and Misconceptions about Photographic Memory
15. The Future of Photographic Memory Research

CHAPTER 1

What is Photographic Memory and How Does it Work

Have you ever been astounded by someone's capacity to vividly recall a substantial amount of information? Have you ever seen someone who is able to recall every little detail of a picture they saw years ago? Or someone who, with only one reading, can memorise entire pages of text? These people are frequently described as having "photographic memory." But what is photographic memory exactly, and how does it function?

Eidetic memory, commonly referred to as photographic memory, is the capacity to vividly recall visual details. People who have this kind of memory frequently refer to it as a **"photograph-like"** memory because they can vividly recall images, colours, and other small visual details. People with photographic memories are able to recall information as if they had an image of it in their minds.

It is the capacity to accurately and precisely recall vivid details of sounds, sights, and other sensory information. People with eidetic memory are able to recall details even after only a brief exposure to them, and frequently claim to be able to visualise past experiences just as vividly as if they were actually there.

It is a talent that is highly valued and frequently linked to brilliance. Research reveals that many people have some degree of eidetic memory, despite the common misconception that it is a gift that only a small number of people possess.

It's vital to keep in mind that not everyone with an extraordinary memory has photographic memory. While some people are born with this talent, others acquire it through practise and training.

How Does Photographic Memory Work?

It is unclear exactly how the photographic memory works. However, research indicates that it might be connected to how the brain interprets and retains visual data. It's thought that people with photographic memories may conjure up extremely detailed mental images and keep them in their long-term memory.

According to one idea, people who have photographic memories have a greater connection between the visual cortex and the hippocampus, which is in charge of storing and retrieving memories. According to another explanation, these people can store visual information in high detail because their encoding and retrieval processes are more effective.

◆ ◆ ◆

CHAPTER 2

Types of Photographic Memory

Let's first talk about the many types of memory and how they function in order to comprehend the various types of photographic memory.

1. Visual Memory

The capacity to recall and remember visual information, such as pictures, shapes, colours, and patterns, is known as visual memory. For photographers, designers, and painters, this kind of remembering is crucial. People with a strong visual memory are able to recall vivid images and scenes with clarity and accuracy.

Iconic memory and eidetic memory are the two types of visual memory.

Iconic memory: The ability to recall an image for a brief period of time, typically less than one second, is referred to as iconic memory. Reading, driving, and sports are just a few activities that frequently require this kind of recall.

Eidetic memory: On the other hand, eidetic memory is the capacity to accurately and vividly recall an image or scene even after it has been obscured from view. Those who have eidetic memory are able to mentally replay scenes as if they were currently in front of them.

2. Auditory Memory

The capacity to retain and remember sounds, voices, and music is known as auditory memory. Sound engineers, singers, and musicians all require this kind of memory. People with a strong auditory memory are able to accurately recall the rhythms, lyrics, and melodies of songs.

Short-term memory and long-term memory are the two types of auditory memory.

Short-term memory: It is the capacity to retain sounds for a small amount of time, typically under 30 seconds. Listening to lectures, chats, and phone calls all require this kind of recall.

Long-term memory: On the other hand, long-term memory refers to the capacity to recall sounds over a longer time frame, occasionally throughout a lifetime. Activities like singing, playing an instrument, and learning music all make use of this kind of memory.

3. Spatial Memory

The capacity to recall spatial information, such as addresses, places, and maps, is known as spatial memory. Pilots, navigators, and explorers all need to have this kind of memory. People with strong spatial memories can recall a building's layout, a city's location, or travel instructions.

Visual-spatial memory and verbal-spatial memory are the two subtypes of spatial memory.

Visual-spatial memory: The capacity to recall spatial information in the form of images and pictures is referred to as visual-spatial memory. Strong visual-spatial memory allows a person to mentally see a city's location or a building's layout in order to recall it.

Verbal-spatial memory: On the other hand, verbal-spatial memory describes the capacity to recall spatial information as words and phrases. Strong verbal-spatial memory allows people to mentally recite directions or locations in order to recall them.

4. Working Memory

The capacity for immediate memory and information manipulation is known as working memory. For tasks like decision-making, multitasking, and problem-solving, this kind of memory is necessary. A person with a good working memory can recall several bits of information at once and use them to solve problems and make decisions.

Short-term working memory and long-term working memory are the two types of working memory.

Short-term working memory refers to the ability to remember and manipulate information for a limited duration, usually less than one minute.

Long-term working memory, on the other hand, refers to the ability to remember and manage information over a longer period, sometimes for days or weeks.

5. Emotional Memory

Emotional memory is the ability to remember and recall emotional experiences, such as joy, sadness, fear, and anger. While emotional memory and photographic memory are not directly related, people with photographic memory may be able to recall emotional memories very precisely and in great detail. For example, they may remember a specific event or situation with vivid clarity, including the emotions that were felt at the time.

It's crucial to keep in mind that not everyone who has a great photographic memory also has a strong emotional memory, and vice versa. Genetics, contextual conditions, and individual experiences are just a few of the variables that have an impact on both types of memory.

Furthermore, emotional memory can affect individuals with or without photographic memory, as emotional experiences are processed and stored differently in the brain compared to other types of memories. Whether or not a person has a photographic memory, emotionally charged events are usually easier to remember and recall than neutral ones.

Types Of Photographic Memory

True eidetic memory and pseudo-eidetic memory are the two primary categories of photographic memory.

True eidetic memory is uncommon and typically only manifests in young children under the age of 12. The ability of these kids to recall images with amazing accuracy and detail is unaffected by distractions or the passage of time, among other things.

Pseudo-eidetic memory: On the other hand, pseudo-eidetic memory is more widespread and can be improved with practise. Although persons with pseudo-eidetic memory can recall vivid details of visuals, their recall capacity is typically less than that of those with actual eidetic memory.

◆ ◆ ◆

CHAPTER 3

*How to Develop a
Photographic Memory*

Have you ever wished you had an unfailing memory? Many people would want to have the ability to remember everything they see and hear with absolute clarity. The good news is that with sufficient effort and the right techniques, you can become a memory expert.

It is crucial to understand that while certain people may naturally have a photographic memory, this superpower is not unique to a small group of people. Anyone can learn how to acquire a photographic memory with sufficient practise.

Improving Your Memory Retention

Before getting into particular methods for improving your photographic memory, it's important to comprehend how memory retention functions.

Information must be encoded, saved, and then retrieved in

order for memory retention to occur. The brain does these tasks through a variety of processes.

1. **Encoding** is the initial phase, which entails transforming sensory data into a format that the brain can understand and store.
2. The information is then **stored** in the brain for potential recall in the second stage.
3. The stored data is returned to the conscious mind for use in the third stage, **retrieval**.

You can take part in activities that encourage these three phases to enhance memory retention. Several methods that work include:

Paying attention: The information you wish to remember needs to be the centre of your attention. The information will not be properly encoded if you are preoccupied or not paying attention.

Rehearsal: You may improve your memory by telling yourself the details repeatedly. The short-term memory benefits most from this method.

Association: It can be easier to remember new knowledge if you connect it to something you already know. You can associate the names and recall the new person's name more easily, for instance, if you meet someone named John and you have a friend with the same name.

Techniques To Develop Photographic Memory

While some people have photographic memories from birth, this ability can be developed with practise.

Here are some methods that could be useful:

Visualization

Start by mentally imagining the details you wish to remember in order to develop a photographic memory. If you're having trouble remembering a phone number, for instance, see the numbers as though they were printed out in front of you.

Association

Associating the knowledge with something you already know is an additional method for improving your photographic memory. For instance, if you're having trouble remembering someone's name, connect it to a picture that symbolises their name.

Repetition

Repetition is a tried-and-true technique for aiding memory. Repeat the information repeatedly until it is etched in your brain to create a photographic memory.

Memory exercises

Games and puzzles that require memory are also helpful in improving photographic memory. Try learning a deck of cards or a list of random numbers, for instance.

❖ ❖ ❖

CHAPTER 4

*Techniques to Improve Your
Photographic Memory*

You may develop your memory recall skills by training your brain. The following methods can help you sharpen your photographic memory.

1. Pay Attention to Details

Paying attention to details is the first tip for enhancing your photographic memory. This means that you should concentrate on the details that you want to recall and make an effort to visualise them. You can remember more specifics about something the more focus you give it. You can use this method to help you recall anything, including names, faces, and scenes.

2. Create Mental Images

The second method involves visualising things in your head. This means that you should make an effort to mentally picture the details you wish to recall. For instance, you could attempt to mentally picture the numbers of a phone number if you wish to remember it. This method can also be used to recall people's names or looks. Try to visualise the person's name or face in your head and link it to a simple-to-remember memory trigger.

3. Use Mnemonics

Another method you can use to sharpen your photographic memory is mnemonics. Mnemonics are tools for improving memory by linking information with something else. As an illustration, you can use an acronym to make it easier for you to remember the items on a list. You can use mnemonics to help you recall anything, including names, dates, and facts.

4. Practice Visualization

You may enhance your photographic memory by using the technique of visualisation. The act of visualising involves forming mental pictures in your head. You can utilise visualisation to help you recall any information you need, including facts, names, and scenes. The more you visualise things, the simpler it is to recall information.

5. Use Association Techniques

Another strategy for enhancing your photographic memory is association. Using this method, you link important information with something else that is simple to recall. For instance, if you want to remember a name, you can connect it to a well-known figure or thing. You can use this method to help you remember anything, including dates, phone numbers, and facts.

6. Play Memory Games

It's enjoyable and helpful to play memory games to develop your visual memory. Playing memory games might help you recall information more easily and challenge your brain. Memory games can be played offline or online with friends and family. Card matching, word association, and puzzle games are a few of the most well-liked memory games.

7. Chunking

Chunking is a method that entails dividing information into smaller, easier-to-manage chunks. You can break up a long string of information into manageable parts rather than trying to recall it all at once.

For instance, you can divide a large string of digits like 437189230 into smaller chunks like 43-71-89-23-0 rather than trying to recall them all at once. This breaks the number up into manageable chunks rather than a big string, making it simpler to recall.

8. Mind Mapping

A visual memory technique called mind mapping entails drawing a layout of the data you want to retain. By placing the main concept in the middle of a piece of paper and then branching out with related concepts, you can create a mind map.

Tips To Maintain Photographic Memory

It's crucial to preserve your photographic memory after you've acquired it. Here are some pointers to assist:

1. Practice regularly:

Keep strengthening the above-mentioned skills to keep your photographic memory sharp.

2. Stay focused:

When it comes to photographic memory, focus is essential. Distractions should be avoided in order to focus on the information you wish to recall.

3. Get enough sleep:

For the consolidation of memories, sleep is crucial. To keep your photographic memory sharp, make sure you receive adequate sleep.

4. Exercise:

Exercise has been demonstrated to enhance memory and cognitive performance. Make frequent exercise a part of your regimen to keep your photographic memory sharp.

◆ ◆ ◆

CHAPTER 5

Memory Palace: A technique for remembering anything

The Memory Palace, often called the Method of Loci, is a memory-improving mnemonic technique. The method entails connecting information to precise places in a well-known setting, such a home or building. By doing this, the data is organised and made simpler to remember by mentally traversing the Memory Palace.

Follow the steps below to employ the Memory Palace technique:

1. Choose a familiar place:

Choose a place you are familiar with, such as your home, workplace, or place of education.

2. Create a mental image:

Make a mental image of the location and identify specific features or items in each location.

3. Associate information with each location:

Select the details you wish to keep in mind and link them to each location. To recall a list of items, for instance, you may assign each item to a particular space or thing in your Memory Palace.

4. Walk through the Memory Palace:

Walk through your Memory Palace in your head, remembering the details related to each spot. To make the associations stronger, try to picture yourself engaging with the material at each location.

You can enhance your memory recall and make it simpler to retain knowledge for exams, presentations, and other tasks by using the Memory Palace technique. It is particularly helpful for recalling lists, speeches, or significant dates. You can refine your Memory Palace and turn it into a useful tool for remembering the information with some practise.

◆ ◆ ◆

CHAPTER 6

Mnemonic devices for memorization

A nyone looking to improve their memory, even those with photographic memories, might benefit from using mnemonic devices.

Here are a few instances:

Acronyms:

Utilising the first letter of each item you want to remember, create an acronym. To recall the placement of the planets in our solar system, for instance: My very eager mother just served us nine pizzas (Mercury, Venus, Earth, Mars, Jupiter, Saturn, Uranus, Neptune, Pluto).

Visualization:

Make a mental picture of the information you wish to recall. Make it as detailed and as colourful as you can. Imagine yourself putting each item on your grocery list in your cart as you travel through the supermarket, for instance, to help you remember it.

Rhyming:

To help you recall information, come up with a rhyme or melody. For instance, to remember how many days are in each month, remember that September, April, June, and November all have 30 days; the rest have 31 days, with the exception of February, which has 28 days (or 29 in a leap year).

Chunking:

Information should be divided up into manageable, smaller sections. For instance, divide a phone number into groups of three or four digits to make it easier to recall.

Association:

Make a mental connection between the thing you wish to remember and another thing. To recall someone's name, for instance, correlate it with a word that rhymes with it or a physical trait they have.

It's significant to remember that not everyone can benefit from mnemonic devices. Try out various methods to see which one suits you the best. Additionally, even while mnemonic devices might be useful, you shouldn't use them as your only memory-aid. Repetition and practise are also crucial for memory retention.

◆ ◆ ◆

CHAPTER 7

How to Remember Names and Faces

You can apply a few general strategies to strengthen your memory for names and faces.

Focus on the person:

When you first meet someone, look closely at their face and try to identify any distinguishing characteristics that will help you remember them. Examine their mouth, nose, and any other identifying characteristics, such as their eyes.

Repeat the name:

Recite someone's name back to them after being introduced, and try to use it in conversation. This will aid in committing the name to memory.

Use visualization:

Make an association between the person's name and face in your memory. For instance, if you meet someone with the name "Rose," picture a rose in their hair or on their lapel.

Associate names with something familiar:

Immediately connect the person's name to someone or something you are familiar with. For instance, if you run into someone named "Samantha," picture Samantha from "Bewitched" on television.

Make a connection:

Look for a distinguishing feature or characteristic that you can connect with the person's name. For instance, you can connect someone's name to their particular haircut.

Practice:

The more you do it, the easier it will get to remember people's names and faces. Make an attempt to employ these strategies frequently, and you'll discover that remembering names and faces gets much simpler with time.

It's vital to remember that efficient name and face recall does not require photographic memory. You may strengthen your memory and get better at retaining the details of the individuals you meet with practise and the use of strategies like those mentioned above.

❖ ❖ ❖

CHAPTER 8

How to Remember Dates and Numbers

Here are some general strategies that might aid in your ability to recall dates and numbers.

Chunking:

Make smaller groupings of digits from lengthy numbers or dates. You can simplify a difficult number, like 123456789, so that it is simpler to remember. For instance, you can recall 123-456-789 rather than 123456789.

Acronyms:

By utilising the first letter of each phrase or number you want to remember, create an acronym. For instance, you can use the acronym PEMDAS to recall the mathematical order of operations (Parentheses, Exponents, Multiplication, Division, Addition, Subtraction).

Visualization:

Associate the number or date you want to recall with mental pictures. For instance, you can picture Christopher Columbus discovering America in 1492 if you wish to recall the date.

Association:

Make a connection between the number or date you wish to remember and another, more memorable thing. For instance, you can link each digit of a phone number to a person or thing you are familiar with in order to remember it.

Repetition:

To assist you remember the number or date, repeat it numerous times. To help you remember it, you can also put it in writing or speak it aloud.

Memory palace:

Build a memory palace by linking each number or date with a specific location in a familiar setting, such as your house or place of employment. Then, to remember the location, you mentally navigate there.

Always keep in mind that certain strategies will be more effective for you than for someone else.

◆ ◆ ◆

CHAPTER 9

How to Remember Text and Information

You can increase the amount of text and information you can recall in your memory by using certain general approaches.

Visualization:

Try to visualise what you read or hear when you are reading or listening to it. This can aid in improving your recall of the specifics.

Association:

Make an effort to link the information you want to remember to something you already know. A vivid image, a sound, a mood, a personal experience, a rhyme, or anything else that can inspire a connection can serve as this.

Repetition:

Repeating something a few times will help it stick in your

memory.

Chunking:

Divide the content into manageable, more compact sections. It may be simpler to recall and remember as a result.

Mindfulness:

Being conscious as you learn or study might aid in maintaining focus and improving memory.

Use Memory Palace technique:

With this method, information is linked to specific locations in a familiar setting. It's similar to making an internal informational map.

Active recall:

Check your answers to ensure accuracy after recalling the information from memory without looking at it.

Mnemonic devices:

To aid with memory, use a mnemonic technique like an acronym, rhyme, or acrostic.

Spaced repetition:

In order to give your brain enough time to organise the

information into long-term memory, review the material at increasingly longer intervals.

Practice:

Regularly practising these approaches will help you retain information better over time.

Keep in mind that memory is a complicated and individualised process, so what is effective for one person may not be effective for another. It's crucial to try out various methods in order to determine which one suits you the most.

◆ ◆ ◆

CHAPTER 10

Photographic Memory and Education

Any skill can be developed more easily in children than in adults. From an early age, developing and exercising photographic memory can have various advantages, including:

1. Retention of information:

Students with photographic memories are better able to retain material for extended periods of time because they can recall it with remarkable accuracy and detail. This can be especially helpful in courses like science and history where it's important to memorise facts and figures.

2. Improved learning speed:

The ability to recall information accurately allows pupils with photographic memories to absorb and digest information more quickly than others. This can be especially helpful in topics like foreign language vocabulary where there is a lot of memorising required.

3. Better test-taking ability:

On assessments when the ability to recall particular details or facts is required, those with photographic memories may have an advantage. They are stronger at recalling facts fast and precisely, which can help them perform better on tests.

4. Enhanced creativity:

Students with photographic memory may be better able to think creatively and generate original ideas because it frequently requires a great capacity to visualise and retain images. This can be very helpful while studying areas like art and design.

5. Improved problem-solving skills:

Children who have photographic memory may find it easier to visualise and comprehend difficult ideas, which can improve their capacity for critical thought and problem-solving.

6. Improved social skills:

Children with photographic memories may retain specifics about people and events, which can strengthen their relationships with others and improve their ability to function in social situations.

7. Increased confidence:

Growing up with a photographic memory can give kids a strong feeling of self-worth and the confidence to believe in their abilities.

◆ ◆ ◆

A child's photographic memory may be trained and practised from an early age, which can have a variety of advantages that can help them succeed in school, be more outgoing and creative as adults, and generally improve their quality of life.

Activities To Train Children In Photographic Memory

The following activities can assist kids in developing photographic memory:

1. Memory games:

Children can enhance their recall skills by playing one of the various memory games that are available. You may, for instance, use a deck of cards and ask your kid to learn the cards' positions in memory. As an alternative, you might have your kid remember where each card is on a board in a memory matching game.

2. Picture books:

Help your child look at picture books and try to remember the specifics of each illustration. You might quiz them on what they observed and encourage them to recall certain specifics.

3. Drawing and coloring:

By making them focus on details, drawing and colouring might help kids strengthen their visual memory abilities. Encourage your kid to colour or draw from memory before comparing the result to the original picture.

4. Observation exercises:

Asking your child questions about the features they noticed after having them focus on an object for a predetermined amount of time will help you practise observation skills with them.

5. Memory challenges:

Test your child's memory after having them memorise a run of numbers, a list of words, or a collection of pictures. As their abilities advance, gradually increase the challenges' level of difficulty.

To encourage kids to practise and develop their skills, be sure to make these activities enjoyable and interesting for them.

◆ ◆ ◆

CHAPTER 11

*Photographic Memory and
Career Advancement*

A photographic memory can help you develop in your profession in a number of ways, including:

1. Improved Learning and Retention:

An individual with photographic memory can quickly understand and memorise vast amounts of information. This can be especially helpful in industries like medicine, law, engineering, or any other job requiring a broad knowledge base.

2. Better Problem-Solving Abilities:

The ability to recall details or patterns that may be essential to figuring out a solution is another way that photographic memory might aid in the resolution of difficult issues.

3. Increased Creativity:

The ability to vividly visualise and recall thoughts or images can help someone's creativity by inspiring them to come up with original and creative solutions.

4. More Efficient Time Management:

People with photographic memories may retain crucial details and information without having to look it up. In the workplace, this can increase effectiveness and productivity.

5. Enhanced Communication Skills:

By helping someone remember names, faces, and specifics of discussions, photographic memory can also improve communication skills and increase one's ability to network and form relationships.

Careers In Which Photographic Memory Plays A Major Role

Although it is not a requirement for any profession, it can be helpful in a variety of fields. Following are a few professions where having a photographic memory could be crucial:

1. Crime Scene Investigator:

Recalling the specifics of a crime scene, such as the position of the evidence, the suspect's appearance, and other significant facts, may be aided by having a photographic memory.

2. Medical Professional:

The specifics of a patient's medical history, test results, and diagnostic imaging could be remembered by a doctor or nurse with a photographic memory.

3. Archivist or Historian:

When it comes to remembering the specifics of historical events, facts, and data, a photographic memory may be quite helpful.

4. Artist or Designer:

Using their recollection of diverse things, scenes, or people, a photographer, graphic designer, or artist with a photographic memory could produce extremely accurate and detailed photographs.

5. Language Interpreter:

Language interpreters with photographic memories would be better able to retain specifics of talks, dialects, and accents.

6. Sports Analyst or Coach:

A photographic memory might be helpful for planning plays, memorising game specifics, and evaluating an athlete's performance.

7. Musician:

A musician with a photographic memory could effortlessly learn and play challenging parts of music.

8. Mathematician:

Formulas, equations, and mathematical ideas would be effortlessly recalled by a mathematician with a photographic memory.

9. Law:

Legal professionals with photographic memories can recall a wealth of case law and other legal precedent, which is helpful in courtroom arguments. Large portions of legal papers, such contracts and briefs, can also be memorised by them.

10. Business:

In the business environment, where CEOs and business owners frequently need to recall a lot of information fast, photographic memory can be useful. People with photographic memories may retain crucial information, like financial statistics, market trends, and business strategy, very rapidly.

Although having a photographic memory can be helpful in some professions, it is also critical to develop a wide range of talents and to concentrate on establishing a solid professional reputation via hard work, commitment, and constant learning.

❖ ❖ ❖

CHAPTER 12

The Science Behind Photographic Memory

The brain is vital to the generation and recall of memories, according to research. The brain records new experiences as memory traces by encoding the information. This trace is then kept in the hippocampus, amygdala, and prefrontal cortex, among other parts of the brain.

The visual cortex of the brain is crucial in processing and storing visual data in the case of visual memory. The processing of different forms of visual information, such as colour, shape, and motion, is specialised in various parts of the visual cortex.

Although the precise mechanics underlying photographic memory are still not fully understood, researchers have found a number of potential contributing elements. These consist of:

Neural connections:

According to studies, those with photographic memories have more neural connections in the visual cortex and other parts of the brain. They could be able to process and remember visual information more quickly as a result.

Attention:

Those with photographic memories tend to focus on the specifics of the information they are trying to remember. They could be able to produce more vivid, simple-to-recall mental images as a result.

Encoding:

People with photographic memories are thought to have a different method of storing sensory information into memory. For instance, they can choose a more visual encoding technique to help them remember images more quickly.

Retrieval:

People with photographic memories may retrieve information more quickly and accurately by taking a more direct path when recalling data from memory.

According to several research, people with good memories may have different brain structures than average that help them remember things. For instance, one study discovered that the temporal lobes, a part of the brain involved in memory and emotion processing, were larger in those with significantly superior autobiographical memory.

Overall, it is obvious that the brain plays a crucial part in encoding, storing, and recalling memories of all types, including visual memories, even though the brain's functions in photographic memory are still poorly understood.

◆ ◆ ◆

CHAPTER 13

World Records done using Photographic Memory

P hotographic memory has been used to set a number of amazing world records. Here are a few examples.

The most digits of pi memorized:

Akira Haraguchi of Japan holds the record for memorising the most pi digits, having recited 100,000 of them in 2006. In groups of 100, he memorised the digits using his photographic memory.

The most decks of cards memorized:

Alex Mullen of the United States holds the record for memorising the most decks of cards, memorising 21 decks (1,568) in one hour in 2016. He remembered the arrangement of the cards with the photographic memory he possessed.

The most names and faces memorized:

Marlo Knight of the United States holds the record for memorising the most names and faces in 15 minutes, having memorised 219 names and faces in 2019. She could recall the specifics of each person's face and name thanks to her photographic memory.

The most binary digits memorized:

Rajveer Meena of India holds the record for memorising the most binary digits, memorising 70,000 of them in a single hour in 2020. He remembered the binary code for each digit with the photographic memory he was known for.

The most words memorized in one hour:

Andi Bell of the United Kingdom holds the record for memorising the most words in an hour (1,028 random words in one hour in 2012). He remembered the words in the right order because to his photographic memory.

❖ ❖ ❖

CHAPTER 14

Myths and Misconceptions about Photographic Memory

Photographic memory is the subject of numerous myths and misconceptions, some of which have been fueled by media such as films and television. Some of the most typical are listed below:

Photographic memory is always accurate:

Photographic memory people frequently recall images in amazing detail, but these memories are not always reliable. Eidetic memory can be impacted by things like distraction, suggestion, and the passage of time, just like any other sort of memory.

Photographic memory is always visual:

Some eidetic memory people may also have strong auditory or olfactory recollections, while most have strong visual memories.

Photographic memory is a superpower:

Although having a photographic memory is unquestionably impressive, it is not a superpower. The way some people's brains process and store information varies from others.

Everyone with photographic memory can remember everything perfectly:

Although those with photographic memories may be remarkably good at recalling visual details, they are nonetheless susceptible to mistakes in remembering and forgetting. In fact, according to some studies, those who have photographic memories may be more prone to false recollections than those who don't.

Photographic memory is always an advantage:

Even though having an excellent memory can be useful in many aspects of life, those who have photographic memories may also encounter some drawbacks, such as trouble forgetting upsetting or emotional situations.

Photographic memory is the same as eidetic memory:

Although the phrases are occasionally used synonymously, photographic memory and eidetic memory are not the same thing. Photographic memory is the capacity to remember images with a high level of accuracy and detail for a prolonged period of time, while eidetic memory refers to the capacity to maintain an image in visual memory for a brief duration after the image has been withdrawn.

Even if the subject of photographic memory is intriguing, it's crucial to distinguish fact from fantasy while talking about this talent.

◆ ◆ ◆

CHAPTER 15

The Future of Photographic Memory Research

There has been a long-running investigation of photographic memory, but the findings have been contradictory. While some studies have revealed little to no evidence of photographic memory, others have indicated that some people have the capacity to retain visual information with amazing accuracy.

Understanding the brain processes underlying photographic memory is one area of ongoing research. It is now possible to analyse the brain activity of those who claim to have photographic memories because of advancements in brain imaging technology. These investigations may aid in locating the brain areas and neural networks involved in the storage and retrieval of visual information.

Another field of study seeks to create methods for increasing memory and the recall of visual information. This study might be useful in areas like education, where higher memory retention could result in better learning outcomes.

Overall, technological and neurological developments are expected to influence photographic memory studies in the future. Researchers may be able to create more potent methods for increasing memory and recall of visual information if they obtain a better grasp of the brain systems behind memory.

❖ ❖ ❖

ABOUT THE AUTHOR

V. Aishwaryalakshmi

Thank you for joining me in exploring the fascinating world of photographic memory! This book has been hard work, but also very enjoyable. I am positive that these memory tips will come handy in your daily life. I am an independent author living in Chennai, India who, apart from writing enjoys travelling and exploring places.

Printed in Great Britain
by Amazon